Spanish Short Stories for Beginners: ***Learn Spanish by Reading and Improve Your Vocabulary***

1. edition: 2018

Independently published

ISBN: 978-3-9822692-7-6

SPANISH SHORT STORIES FOR BEGINNERS

Learn Spanish by Reading and Improve Your Vocabulary

Marta Torres Sánchez

Table of Contents

Bonus – 10 Free Exercises

We've compiled ten exercises for you, two for each story: the first exercise will allow you to ingrain new vocabulary you will acquire through each story, while the second one focuses on grammar points that are relevant at the beginner's level A1/A2. At the end of each exercise, there are also the correct answers.

Instructions For Downloading The Free Exercises

To download the exercises, go to the following link:

http://bit.ly/free-spanish-exercises

(You should access the link on your smartphone or computer to view to or download the exercises.)

On the dedicated site, please enter your email address and your name. Then, click "DOWNLOAD".

Go to the inbox of the email address you've just entered. Find the email sent from Bono Digital with the subject "Please Confirm Your Subscription". If you cannot find the email, please also check your Spam or Promotions folders.

Once you've confirmed your email address by clicking the button "CONFIRM YOUR EMAIL", you will receive a new email with the subject line "Here are your free Spanish exercises!". Clicking the link in the email (or the picture of the book) will instantly give you access to your free exercises!

You can do the exercises immediately or you can download the file by clicking the download button (in the upper right-hand corner) and print it, if you wish.

If you encounter any problems, you can contact us at the email address you find at the back of this book – we'll do our best to help you out.

Enjoy!

INTRODUCTION

Congratulations for buying *"Spanish Short Stories for Beginners: Learn Spanish by Reading and Improve Your Vocabulary."*

Nelson Mandela once said that when you talk to a man in his own language, the message will go straight to his heart. If this is true, then you'll have the power to touch more than 470 million hearts once you understand and speak Spanish. It is the second most spoken language in the world based on the number of native speakers. That's why learning Spanish is not only fun, but also practical.

Spanish is the official language in 20 countries worldwide and international organizations like the United Nations, European Union, and the World Trade Organization. The Hispanic Monarchy used to be the largest empire in the world. Between the 15th and 19th century, Spain ruled a huge portion of America, the Asian archipelago of the Philippines and some territories in Europe, Oceania and Africa. The colonizers infused their religion, culture and language into these places.

Besides Spain, most Spanish speakers live in Hispanic America and the Central African nation of

Equatorial Guinea. Spanish-speaking nations in the Americas include Argentina, Belize, Bolivia, Chile, Colombia, Costa Rica, Cuba, Dominican Republic, Ecuador, El Salvador, Guatemala, Honduras, Mexico, Nicaragua, Panama, Paraguay, Peru, Puerto Rico, Uruguay and Venezuela. There are also many Spanish speakers in the U.S.A., especially in states near Mexico. Furthermore, millions from around the world use Spanish as a second language. In fact, it is considered as the third most spoken language by the total number of speakers (native and non-native).

Why Learn Spanish?

Knowledge of Spanish is an important asset for those who travel or engage in business. It is the language of trade in Spain and Latin America, where most businessmen speak Spanish exclusively. The Hispanic market is fast-growing and one of the largest in the world. Even in the U.S., the world's biggest economy, there are large communities where Spanish is prominently spoken.

It is the culture of Hispanic people to get to know their business partners and associates. Knowing how to speak their language builds strong professional ties. People with different careers also benefit from learning Spanish as a foreign language. If you want to work in a Spanish-speaking country or community, expect that most people could have a limited English vocabulary. Having a good grasp of Spanish eliminates problems in communication.

This is also true when you're travelling. Spain is a dream destination for many tourists and for good reasons. The interesting mix of Catholic and Moorish influence on Spain's culture is captured in its treasure chest of art and architecture. Its history resonates in well-preserved towns, churches, palaces, and monasteries. Costa del Sol, in the South of Spain, hosts spectacular views of turquoise seas and white-walled villages.

The good thing about learning Spanish is that you can use it in many other destinations. You can find equally impressive travel experiences in Spain's former colonies. Ancient cities, dense jungles and immaculate beaches are also waiting to be explored in Latin America. Speaking Spanish increases your travel experience manifold. By engaging with the locals, you'll be able to immerse in the rich Hispanic culture. Hispanic people are known to be proud of their heritage, and eager to share it with others.

If you're not planning to travel to any Spanish-speaking country soon, knowing the language is still useful to connect with people. Spanish is the third most spoken language in the internet. In an increasingly borderless world brought by technology, learning another language is beneficial to anyone.

Is Spanish Hard to Learn?

Spanish is relatively easy to learn. Its grammar is objectively straightforward, lacking the complexities of languages such as Russian or Chinese. It also has fewer exceptions than English or French. Spanish is easy to pronounce. Many words in its vocabulary are recognizable by English speakers. The challenging aspects in learning Spanish are word genders and conjugation.

Spanish is a good gateway lingo towards becoming a polyglot. It is closely similar to Italian, Catalan, Portuguese and French. If you already know Spanish, you can understand large chunks of these languages without even studying them. In the U.S., Spanish is the most popular second language learned.

There are slight variations and differences in accent across Spanish-speaking countries. This occurs when a language develops in isolation from its source. Don't worry. The differences in different Spanish accent won't pose many problems. You will still understand what most natives are saying with little difficulty.

How to Learn a Foreign Language Fast

If you want to learn a foreign language fast, it's important that you put equal effort in developing the four skills of language learning. Developing these skills will help you develop your comprehension, and at the same time, set you up to become an effective communicator. Think about how you learned your first language. Usually, it's the listening skills that develop first, then speaking, then reading and writing. Here's a brief description of the 4 capabilities, or the LSRW skills.

Listening – the first skill that we learn in our native language. Known as a passive or receptive skill, listening involves receiving language through our ears, and allowing the brain to make sense of what was said. While listening is said to be the mother of all language skills, not many people put enough effort into developing their listening skills.

The best way to practice is to familiarize yourself with as much native sources of language as you can. Watch Spanish movies (with or without the subtitles) and listen to Spanish podcasts and audiobooks. Try listening purely for the different sounds first before you start looking for the context of the material you're listening to.

Speaking – the second skill that we learn in our native language. Speaking is an active or productive skill that involves using our vocal tract to produce language that our brain has interpreted. Speaking is often the number one weakness for anyone acquiring a second language as it is common for us to start learning a language through reading.

One way to improve your speaking skill is to read text out loud. Practice reading along with a recording at first, then reread the text on your own, but this time, pay attention to the pronunciation and the inflections on the sentences.

Notice that Spanish pronunciation is different from the English pronunciation so practice making the correct sounds. Reading aloud activates your mouth and diaphragm's muscle memory and helps you get used to saying unfamiliar words out loud.

Reading – It may be the third skill that we learn from our native language, but reading is the first skill that we learn in acquiring a new language.

Reading is a passive or receptive skill that involves using our eyes and brains to understand written language.

Reading in a foreign language is important because it effectively exposes you to more words and sentences than listening to a song or watching a movie. Your brain is more receptive to accepting brain feed (grammar patterns, vocabulary words) through reading, so make sure to look for the right reading material for your level. Picking out a difficult reading material early on will only overload your cognitive function and demotivate you from making reading a habit.

Writing – the fourth skill that we learn in our native language, writing is an active or productive skill that involves using our hands and brains to write symbols that represent the spoken language.

Writing in a foreign language is relatively easy if your native language makes use of the same system of writing, but if you're learning a language that uses a different one, like Chinese or Japanese, then you'll need to learn a whole new set of characters and symbols.

Good thing Spanish uses the Roman alphabet so if you can read this, then you shouldn't have any problems writing in Spanish. The best way to improve your writing skills is to read as much as you can. While reading, focus on sentence structure, punctuation, style, and other aspects that will help you get your point across through writing. Read different types of texts and try to replicate them in different scenarios.

While there's no denying the importance of all four language skills in further enhancing our knowledge of our native language, just how important are these skills in learning Spanish? Do you need to master all four to communicate effectively in your second language? Well, the answer is yes and no.

Yes, if you want to eventually be near-native fluent. No, if you're learning goal doesn't involve all four skills. So for example, if you only want to learn Spanish just to survive your next holiday in Spain or South America, writing is not really a priority.

How is Spanish Grammar Taught at Beginners (A1/A2) Levels

The main purpose of this book is to provide you with a challenging and yet entertaining way to help you learn the Spanish language. You'll learn the basics of the Spanish language, from nouns and adjectives to different verb tenses that any beginner will be able to quickly understand. You'll also learn important sentence structures and vocabulary words that will allow you to engage in a casual conversation with a native Spanish speaker. We won't bore you with grammatical notes you'll find in most textbooks. Instead, you'll learn how to use the Spanish language through a more practical method.

If you feel a little bit overwhelmed by this, don't be! Only grammatical aspects appropriate for the A1/A2 levels are included in this book. We've decided to take away the advanced grammatical aspects and tenses so as not to confuse you. The vocabulary is also pretty basic so that beginners such as yourself won't have a hard time understanding the stories.

Guidelines on How to Read the Following Short Stories

We want to help you learn Spanish in the fastest and most convenient way possible. Through this book of compiled stories, we hope to entertain you, and at the same time, ensure that you understand the Spanish language better.

Here are a few guidelines to help you take full advantage of the short stories in this book:

First, try to read through the entire text without checking the meaning of unknown words. Don't feel pressured to recognize all the words from the stories. It's perfectly normal for beginners to recognize only a few words.

After reading the text, try to summarize what you've read based on your initial understanding. You can check if you understood correctly by looking at the short summary at the end of each story. Again, don't feel pressured to get it right on the first try.

Give it another go! Reread the chapter, but this time, concentrating on the words and sentence structure. Try to find the context of the text you're reading. Look for words that seem similar to a language that you're already familiar with. Take note that vocabulary words for that specific text are intentionally repeated in order to give you a better chance to familiarize yourself to them.

Check the glossary of difficult or advanced vocabulary words at the end each story. If you want to consult other materials to help you understand the story better, feel free to do so. You can search the internet for helpful text or read textbooks to get additional information.

At the end of every story, you'll find a set of questions that will help test your comprehension. We encourage you to answer these questions so that you can assess for yourself how well you understood the story.

¡*Que te diviertas*! (Have fun!)

THE STORIES

1. Un Nuevo Trabajo Para Mariana

Mariana es diseñadora gráfica y busca trabajo en alguna compañía de diseño en su zona. Envió varias **solicitudes de empleo** a las empresas de diseño **cercanas** y espera pronto tener respuesta.

Hace una semana, Mariana recibió una llamada de una compañía que se dedica al diseño industrial. La invitan a una **entrevista de trabajo**.

Hoy es la entrevista y Mariana **acaba de** entrar a la oficina del Sr. González, quien está hablando por teléfono...

<u>Sr. González:</u> Pase, pase (dirigiéndose a Mariana) ...

¡No, no y no! (Al **interlocutor** en el teléfono) No voy a pagar por ese trabajo incompleto...

Siéntese por favor (otra vez hablando con Mariana) ...

Pues llámeme cuando tenga una solución (le dice finalmente a la persona en el teléfono y **cuelga**).

(El Sr. González **se pone de pie** para **estrechar la mano** de Mariana...)

Sr. González: ¡Buenas tardes! ¡Qué bueno que está aquí! Nos gusta mucho su CV. Ya la lista de candidatos es de solo tres y usted es uno de ellos.

Mariana: ¡Buenas tardes! ¡Un placer conocerlo!

(El Sr. González vuelve a sentarse en su puesto **tras** el escritorio y se pone a revisar una **carpeta**)

Sr. González: ... A ver... Por favor, hábleme un poco **acerca de** usted.

Mariana: Bueno, tengo 25 años, trabajo como secretaria en un banco desde hace 7 años y así pagué mis estudios en la "Academia de Diseño Arte Nuevo". Mis notas están entre las más altas de la academia y mis trabajos ganaron varios premios en los concursos que se hacen para los estudiantes.

Sr. González: Veo aquí que no menciona su **estado civil** en su solicitud.

Mariana: Bueno, eso es porque los formularios no tienen la opción "separada y en trámites de divorcio". No **quise** poner "casada" porque ya pronto, en unos meses, eso no será verdad.

Sr. González: ... Ya veo. ¿También piensa **mudarse** de donde vive ahora cuando se divorcie?

Mariana: No. La **dirección** que puse es la de mis padres y por un buen tiempo me **quedaré** con ellos. No quiero vivir sola y ellos tienen espacio en su casa...

Sr. González: ... Entiendo. Su expediente como estudiante es verdaderamente fantástico, pero veo que no tiene experiencia laboral como diseñadora.

Mariana: Bueno, no tengo **trabajo fijo** como diseñadora, pero hago **trabajo a destajo** en internet, en esos sitios web en los que se buscan empleados free lance. La verdad, me va muy bien. Es un trabajo que hago en casa, a la hora que mejor me parece y me pagan bien.

Sr. González: ¿Por qué entonces busca trabajo fijo?

Mariana: Tengo muchas buenas razones para buscar un trabajo fijo. Quiero tener seguro hospitalario y dental. Quiero tener todas las **ventajas** de un trabajo fijo: las vacaciones pagadas, el **bono navideño**, la **caja de ahorros** ... usted sabe ... Además, aunque le **parezca** raro, me gusta levantarme temprano, vestirme bien y ponerme bonita para salir a la calle, a estar con gente real...

Sr. González: No, no me parece raro. La entiendo perfectamente. Mi prima sólo trabaja desde su casa y está más gorda. Trabajar cerca del refrigerador de casa es un problema. También es menos cuidadosa con su **arreglo personal**... como no tiene que ver a nadie ...

Mariana: ¡Exacto! Yo soy una persona social. Me gusta tener gente alrededor, me gusta hacer amigos. El trabajo desde casa tiene ventajas, pero es muy **aislado**.

Sr. González: Si obtiene este empleo, ¿piensa **seguir** haciendo trabajo free lance en internet?

Mariana: ... pues la verdad no sé. ¿Por qué lo pregunta?

Sr. González: Bueno... voy a ser sincero y directo con usted, Mariana. Me preocupa que pueda reutilizar nuestras creaciones en otros trabajos. El diseño es un trabajo artístico con aplicaciones prácticas y la creatividad, las nuevas ideas y el impacto que puedan tener nuestros diseños, dependen en mucho de la confidencialidad de nuestros **empleados**. Si le damos el empleo, por ninguna razón puede usted usar las creaciones de nuestra compañía en su trabajo a destajo.

Mariana: Por eso, no se preocupe. Soy una persona honesta. Nunca usaré los diseños de la compañía en ningún otro lugar. Es más, ni siquiera hablaré de ellos...

Sr. González: ¿Firmará usted un **acuerdo de confidencialidad**?

Mariana: ¡Claro que sí!

(El Sr. González se levanta y extiende la mano. Mariana también se levanta y recibe el gesto).

Sr. González: ¡Un verdadero placer conocerla! Si de mí depende, el empleo es suyo, pero debo conversar con mis **socios**...

Mariana: Muchas gracias por todo. Esperemos que sus socios **estén de acuerdo** con usted.

Sr. González: Tomaremos una decisión muy pronto y le **avisaremos** a usted por teléfono.

Mariana: **Se lo agradezco**. Hasta luego.

Sr. González: Hasta luego.

Vocabulario

- **solicitud de empleo** – job application
- **cercano** – nearby, close
- **entrevista de trabajo** – job interview
- **acabar de** (entrar) – has just (entered)
- **interlocutor** – the other person, conversational partner
- **colgar** – hang up (the telephone)
- **ponerse en pie** – to stand up
- **estrechar la mano** – to shake hands
- **tras** – behind
- **carpeta** – folder, file folder
- **acerca** [+de] – about
- **estado civil** – marital status
- **querer** [1ª persona singular (yo) pretérito indicativo: *quise*] – to want, to wish
- **mudarse** – to move away, to relocate
- **dirección** – address
- **quedar** – to stay, to remain
- **trabajo fijo** – steady job
- **trabajo a destajo** – piecework
- **ventaja** – advantage
- **bono navideño** – Christmas bonus
- **caja de ahorros** – savings account

- **parecer** – [3ª persona singular (él/ella/usted) presente subjuntivo: *parezca*] to appear, to seem, to look/sound like
- **arreglo personal** – personal care
- **aislado** – isolated
- **seguir** – continue
- **empleado, empleada** – employee, worker
- **acuerdo de confidencialidad** – non-disclosure agreement
- **socio, socia** – partner, associate
- **estar de acuerdo** – to agree
- **avisar** – to inform, to notify
- **agradecerse** – to express thanks to [sb] for

Resumen

Mariana trabaja en un banco desde hace 7 años. Así pagó sus estudios de diseño industrial. Ahora busca trabajo como diseñadora. Envió varias solicitudes de empleo a algunas compañías de diseño. Mariana recibió una llamada de una compañía de diseño industrial y hoy es el día de la entrevista con el Sr. González de esa compañía. El Sr. González le hace muchas preguntas acerca de su dirección, su estado civil, sus estudios, sus notas y su trabajo a destajo. También le pregunta por qué quiere un trabajo fijo si le va bien en su trabajo como free lance. La entrevista termina y el empleo puede ser para Mariana...

Preguntas de comprensión de la lectura

1. Mariana es
    a. estudiante
    b. diseñadora
    c. académica
    d. banquera

2. Mariana quiere
    a. trabajar en un banco
    b. trabajar como free lance
    c. trabajar en una compañía de diseño
    d. ser estudiante

3. Mariana está
    a. soltera
    b. separada
    c. viuda
    d. divorciada

4. El Sr. González le pregunta a Mariana
    a. su edad
    b. el nombre del banco
    c. los nombres de sus padres
    d. su trabajo a destajo

5. Mariana
   a. trabajará en la compañía de diseño
   b. continuará en el banco
   c. no trabajará más a destajo
   d. recibirá una llamada con la decisión

Respuestas

1. b
2. c
3. b
4. d
5. d

2. El Asalto Al Banco

Hoy en la mañana, dos ladrones **asaltaron** el Banco Regional La Unión que **se encuentra** en el centro comercial "Santa Fe". La policía interroga a varios **testigos** del asalto en la estación de policía. Uno de los oficiales le hace las preguntas del caso a una señora mayor que estuvo presente en el incidente. El oficial, sentado **frente** a su computadora, conversa con la testigo. Luego de escuchar las respuestas, escribe en la computadora y **llena el formulario** de "Declaración de Testigos".

Oficial Montero: Su nombre, por favor.

Sra. Sierra: Elena Sierra.

Oficial Montero: ¿Edad?

Sra. Sierra: 35 años.

(El oficial Montero la mira con severidad y vuelve a preguntar en tono **exigente**)

Oficial Montero: Su edad verdadera, por favor.

Sra. Sierra: ¿Eso es importante?

Oficial Montero: Sí, decir la verdad a la policía es siempre muy importante.

(La Sra. Sierra contesta con actitud resignada.)

Sra. Sierra: 84 años.

Oficial Montero: ¿Cuál es la dirección de su casa?

Sra. Sierra: Avenida "Las Flores", Casa #28, Santa Fe Norte.

Oficial Montero: ¿Estaba usted en el banco cuando ocurrieron los **sucesos**?

Sra. Sierra: ¿Cuáles sucesos?

(El Oficial Montero **contesta** exasperado.)

Oficial Montero: ¡El asalto al banco!

Sra. Sierra: Sí. Fui al banco a **retirar el dinero** que me **enviaron** mis hijos.

Oficial Montero: Vale, ... usted fue al banco en la mañana ... ¿recuerda a qué hora?

Sra. Sierra: Eran como las 10:15 de la mañana.

Oficial Montero: ¿Cómo puede estar tan segura?

Sra. Sierra: Porque, antes de entrar a retirar mi dinero, me tomé un jugo en la cafetería que está junto al banco. Allí escuché las noticias de las 10:00 de la mañana en la radio. Siempre escucho las noticias de las 10:00 en mi móvil. Luego, fui al banco. Unos minutos después entraron los **asaltantes**.

Oficial Montero: ¿Qué fue lo que ocurrió?

Sra. Sierra: Los cuatro bandidos **sacaron** sus armas y **gritaron**: "Esto es un asalto."

Oficial Montero: ¿Está segura de que eran cuatro asaltantes?

Sra. Sierra: Sí. Yo los vi muy bien.

Oficial Montero: El vigilante del banco dice que eran solo dos asaltantes.

Sra. Sierra: ¡Él no se fijó bien!

Oficial Montero: ¿Y dónde estaban los **ladrones**?

Sra. Sierra: Sentados en el **área de espera**, como **todo el mundo**.

Oficial Montero: Y ¿dónde estaba usted?

Sra. Sierra: En la **cola**, esperando ser **atendida** por el **cajero**.

Oficial Montero: ¿Frente de cuál **caja**?

Sra. Sierra: No recuerdo bien.

Oficial Montero: Y las armas ¿cómo eran?

Sra. Sierra: ¡Grandes! Como en las películas.

Oficial Montero: ¿De cañón largo?

Sra. Sierra: Si, muy largo.

Oficial Montero: ¿Le pidieron que se **acostara en el piso**?

Sra. Sierra: Sí, pero les dije que era muy vieja para eso.

Oficial Montero: ¿Puede describirlos?

Sra. Sierra: Sí, eran blancos. Tenían el cabello largo y negro.

Oficial Montero: ¿Blancos? ¿De verdad?

Sra. Sierra: Sí. Eran dos hombres blancos.

Oficial Montero: ¡Pero usted me dijo que eran cuatro asaltantes!

Sra. Sierra: Bueno... es que había dos mujeres también.

Oficial Montero: ¿Dos mujeres? (dice mientras escribe) ¿Y cómo eran las mujeres?

Sra. Sierra: Una era asiática y la otra era morena.

Oficial Montero: Ya veo... ¿Y los dos hombres como **lucían**?

Sra. Sierra: ¿Cuáles hombres?

Oficial Montero: Usted dijo que había dos hombres...

Sra. Sierra: ¡Ah! ¡Sí! Un cajero y un vigilante... pues lucían normales, como siempre lucen los cajeros y los vigilantes.

Oficial Montero: ...mmm (mientras **duda**) ¿Y cómo vestían los asaltantes?

Sra. Sierra: Vestían con **trajes** oscuros y elegantes...

Oficial Montero: ¿Elegantes... como los de las películas?

Sra. Sierra: ¡Ninguna película, señor... era un asalto, por Dios Santo! (dice **subiendo la voz**)

Oficial Montero: Vale, vale, no **se altere**.

En ese momento, entra a la oficina el Jefe Gómez...

Jefe Gómez: ¡Abuela! ¡Qué bueno que viniste! Vamos a llevarte a tu casa.

Sra. Sierra: Vine a ayudarte. Yo fui testigo.

Jefe Gómez: ¿De qué?

Sra. Sierra: ¡Del asalto a la cafetería del centro comercial Santa Fe!

Jefe Gómez: ¿De verdad? Cuéntame.

Sra. Sierra: Pues, eran como las dos de la tarde, hacía calor y entré a la cafetería a tomarme una soda. Luego vino el ladrón... un rubio mal vestido que **olía** muy mal.

Jefe Gómez: (Interrumpiendo) Ya veo. Mejor me sigues contando por el camino...

(La anciana sale y el Jefe Gómez le dice al Oficial Montero) La voy a llevar a su casa...

Oficial Montero: ¿Ella es su abuela, señor?

Jefe Gómez: No..., pero eso cree ella... y bueno, ¡a nadie **hace daño** con esa idea! ¡Ya regreso!

Vocabulario

- **asaltar** – to rob
- **encontrarse** – is located
- **testigo** – witness
- **frente** [+a] – in front of
- **llenar el formulario** – to fill out the form
- **exigente** – demanding, tough
- **suceso** – occurrence, happening, incident
- **contestar** – to answer, to reply
- **retirar (el) dinero** – to withdraw money
- **enviar** – to send
- **asaltante** – thief, robber
- **sacar** – to take out
- **gritar** – to shout, to yell
- **ladrón, ladrona** – thief, robber
- **área de espera** – waiting area
- **todo el mundo** – everybody (lit. *the whole world*)
- **cola** – line, queue
- **atender** – to assist (customers)
- **cajero, cajera** – bank teller, cashier
- **caja** – cash register, register, till
- **acostar en el piso** – to lie down on the floor
- **lucir** – to wear, to dress in
- **dudar** – to doubt
- **traje** – suit

- **subir la voz** – to raise sb's voice
- **alterarse** – to get agitated, upset
- **oler** – to smell, to stink
- **hacer daño** – to hurt, to cause harm

Resumen

Dos ladrones asaltaron un banco y la policía interroga a una anciana que dice ser testigo del asalto. El oficial Montero habla con la testigo en la estación de policía y le pregunta sus datos personales y cómo ocurrió todo. Algunas respuestas de la anciana no son muy lógicas. El oficial Montero no entiende bien lo que la señora está diciendo y comienza a dudar de su testimonio. El jefe de policía interrumpe el interrogatorio y saluda a "su abuela". El oficial Montero pregunta si realmente es la abuela del jefe y éste le dice que no ...

Preguntas de comprensión de la lectura

1. La testigo es:
   a. Una joven de 15 años
   b. Una mujer de 25 años
   c. Una anciana de 84 años
   d. El oficial no se lo pregunta

2. La hora del asalto al banco era:
   a. 08:00 am
   b. 10:15 am
   c. 02:00 pm
   d. 05:00 pm

3. Junto al banco hay un negocio que es:
   a. Una Cafetería
   b. Un supermercado
   c. Una estación de servicio
   d. Una funeraria

4. Los asaltantes eran:
   a. 3 hombres
   b. 2 hombres y 2 mujeres
   c. 2 hombres
   d. 2 mujeres

5. ¿Cuál era la relación entre la anciana y el Jefe Gómez?

a. Era la hermana del Jefe Gómez
b. Era la mamá del Jefe Gómez
c. Era la abuela del Jefe Gómez
d. No tenía relación con el Jefe Gómez

Respuestas

1. c
2. b
3. a
4. c
5. d

3. Una Sonrisa Temible

Jesús es un niño de 8 años que está **mudando sus dientes**. Hoy está visitando al dentista para revisión. Mientras espera su turno para ser examinado, conversa con otro niño de su edad que está **sentado** junto a él.

Jesús: Hola, ¿cómo te llamas?

Pedro: Me llamo Pedro. ¿Cómo te llamas tu?

Jesús: Me llamo Jesús, tengo 8 años y juego fútbol en el colegio.

Pedro: ¡Yo también tengo 8 años! ¡Y yo también juego fútbol en mi colegio! Soy el portero del equipo infantil.

Jesús: Yo juego en la defensa y armo una barrera junto a mis compañeros de equipo. Casi nadie puede **llegar** a nuestra **portería**.

Pedro: Esa barrera es la que yo necesito. La defensa de mi equipo no es muy buena y no **frena** bien a los delanteros. Por eso estoy aquí.

Jesús: ¿Estás aquí porque la defensa de tu equipo no es muy buena? (Jesús dice mientras **se ríe**) ¿Sabes que estás en el **consultorio** de un dentista?

Pedro: (Pedro también se ríe) Ja, ja, ja. Estoy mudando los dientes, pero además me **pegaron con** la **pelota de fútbol** en la cara y me **sacaron** dos dientes que apenas empezaban a **aflojarse**. ¡Mira! (Pedro enseña su boca sin los dos dientes del frente)

Jesús: Lo lamento. ¿Te **duele** mucho?

Pedro: Un poco, pero **aguanto** porque no me gusta que vean al portero del equipo llorando. ¡Debo ser fuerte!

Jesús: Es verdad. Si ven al portero de un equipo llorando creerán que es **débil** y fácil de **batir** en la portería... y eso no es bueno.

Pedro: ¿Y tú por que estas aquí en el dentista?

Jesús: Estoy mudando y algunos dientes nuevos vienen en mala posición. Me los tienen que **arreglar** y ponerme unos aparatos dentales que los **enderezan**.

Pedro: ¿Te van a poner aparatos dentales? ¡Qué bueno! Vas a parecer un robot o un **tiburón**. ¡Yo quiero unos aparatos también!

Jesús: Si, esos **frenillos** son divertidos. Espero que no me duelan.

Pedro: ¡Y si duelen no importa! Vale la pena usarlos y **lucir** diferente, con una sonrisa **temible**. ¡Qué los jugadores del equipo contrario tengan miedo y no **se acerquen** a la portería!

Jesús: Tienes razón. Bastará sonreír y poner "cara de malo" para que los atacantes **se detengan** o **se distraigan** y poder **quitarles** el balón.

Pedro: Voy a pedir que me pongan unos aparatos. ¡Esa será nuestra estrategia!

Jesús: Si, pero ¿qué pasará cuando nuestros equipos **se enfrenten**? Tu y yo sabremos la estrategia y no **caeremos en la trampa** del "aspecto temible".

Pedro: Si acordamos guardar el secreto, esa será nuestra estrategia personal y deportiva y cada uno la usará según le convenga.

Jesús: Entonces hagamos un juramento: "Jesús y Pedro serán temibles dentro y fuera de la **cancha de fútbol** porque tienen una sonrisa macabra... y nadie entenderá que es por los aparatos dentales y la actitud". ¿Lo juras?

Pedro: (con la mano levantada) ¡Lo juro!

Secretaria del dentista: (llamando a Jesús) Jesús Valente, por favor entre al consultorio del doctor.

Pedro: Suerte. Espero verte luego con tu sonrisa macabra.

Jesús: (poniéndose de pie y caminando hacia el consultorio) Gracias. Ya me verás (hace gesto de terror).

Pedro se queda afuera del consultorio jugando con su celular cuando de pronto empieza a escuchar aparatos médicos que suenan y **gritos** de dolor. Pedro **se impresiona** por los **sonidos**, se acerca poco a poco al **regazo** de su madre con cara de miedo. Los gritos se incrementan y Pedro se pone de pie frente a su madre.

Pedro: (a su madre y con voz temblorosa) Mamá, vámonos... me siento mal. ¿Podemos venir otro día?

Madre de Pedro: No Pedro, tenemos **cita** para hoy y no podemos **perderla**.

Los sonidos que vienen desde el consultorio del dentista son cada vez más **aterradores**.

Pedro: (**rogando**) Anda mamá. Vámonos. (Exagerando) ¡Me duele la cabeza y creo que tengo fiebre!

Madre de Pedro: Estás **asustado**, pero no creo que el doctor te vaya a hacer daño.

Pedro: (casi llorando) Sí lo hará. ¡Sí me va a doler!... Y yo juré que... que... no puedo decirlo, pero juré por algo que me va a doler... y ahora no lo quiero.

Madre de Pedro: ¿De qué estás hablando? (Pedro corre hacia la salida) ¿A dónde vas? ¡Pedro... Pedro...!

Vocabulario

- **mudar dientes** – to be losing baby teeth
- **sentado** – sitting, seated
- **llegar** – to arrive, to reach
- **portería** – (football) goal
- **frenar** – to stop
- **reír** – to laugh
- **consultorio** – doctor's office, doctor's practice
- **pegar** – to hit, to strike
- **pelota de fútbol** – (foot)ball
- **sacar** – to remove
- **aflojar** – to loosen
- **doler** – to hurt
- **aguantar** – to hold on, to endure
- **débil** – weak
- **batir** – to beat
- **arreglar** – to repair, to fix, to put in order
- **enderezan** – to straighten
- **tiburón** – shark
- **frenillos** [*Costa Rica, colloquial*] – braces
- **lucir** – to look, to make an impression
- **temible** – fearsome, frightening
- **acercarse** – to get close, to approach
- **detenerse** – to stop, to arrest
- **distraerse** – to get distracted

- **quitar** – to take, to snatch
- **enfrentarse** – to face, to confront
- **caer en la trampa** – to fall into the trap
- **cancha de fútbol** – soccer field, football pitch
- **grito** – cry, scream
- **impresionarse** – to be moved
- **sonido** – sound
- **regazo** – lap, arms
- **cita** – appointment
- **perder** – to lose
- **aterrador** – terrifying, frightening
- **rogar** – to beg, to plead
- **asustado** – frightened, scared

Resumen

Jesús y Pedro son niños a los que les gusta jugar fútbol. Ambos están mudando sus dientes y hoy se encuentran en la sala de espera del dentista para revisión. Mientras esperan su turno, se conocen. Hablan de fútbol, de sus dientes y de un secreto que van a compartir: ambos se van a poner aparatos dentales de corrección para lucir temibles y asustar a sus oponentes del fútbol. Jesús entra al consultorio del dentista y la aplicación de los aparatos dentales le causa dolor. Pedro se asusta con los gritos, no puede aguantar el miedo y corre hacia afuera del consultorio del dentista perseguido por su madre.

Preguntas de comprensión de la lectura:

1. ¿Qué edad tienen Jesús y Pedro?
   a. 7 años
   b. 8 años
   c. 9 años
   d. 10 años

2. ¿Qué posición de fútbol juega Jesús?
   a. Portero
   b. Defensa
   c. Delantero
   d. Entrenador

3. ¿Por qué motivo está Pedro en el dentista?
   a. Porque muda sus dientes
   b. Porque le pegaron con un balón de fútbol en la boca
   c. Porque muda sus dientes y además le pegaron con un balón de fútbol en la boca
   d. Porque es amigo de Jesús

4. ¿Cuál será el efecto de usar aparatos dentales?
   a. Los niños se verán más bonitos
   b. Los niños se verán más interesantes
   c. Los niños se esconderán de sus compañeros

d. Los niños tendrán un aspecto temible

5. Después de escuchar el tratamiento dental de Jesús, Pedro decide:

a. No ponerse los aparatos dentales
b. Ponerse los aparatos dentales
c. Ir a otro dentista
d. No jugar fútbol

Respuestas

1. b
2. b
3. c
4. d
5. a

If you are enjoying this book, would you be kind enough to leave a review for it? It'd be greatly appreciated!

Thank you!

Now, there are two more exciting short stories waiting for you on the following pages!

4. Una Boda De Lujo

Ana y Ramón se casaron hace varios años. Son una joven pareja con empleos, hijos, **mascotas**... y que siempre tienen mucho que hacer. Pero, hoy **pusieron a un lado** su larga lista de obligaciones para **asistir a** una fiesta. Es la recepción de una boda. Luego de **un buen rato** en la fiesta, Ana y Ramón regresan de la boda cansados, pero contentos. Ellos conversan en su habitación mientras **se ponen cómodos** y se relajan...

Ana: (Mientras se deja caer en el **sillón**) ¡Qué buena estuvo esta fiesta! La ceremonia de boda, la música, el salón adornado...

Ramón: Sí, todo estuvo muy bien, sobre todo la cena...

Ana: ¡Y la bebida! ¡Pude tomar champaña toda la noche!

Ramón: Ya vi que te gustó... (Ramón **se quita** la **corbata** y se ríe)

Ana: ¡Es que estaba muy rica! (quitándose los zapatos y **lanzándolos** al armario)

Ramón: La verdad es que creo que nunca **me divertí** tanto en una boda como hoy. De verdad, la pasé muy bien.

Ana: ¡Y pensar que por un momento **dudamos** en ir!

Ramón: (Continúa quitándose la ropa de gala) Casi todas las fiestas de matrimonio están llenas de gente **desconocida**, **chismosa** y **fanfarrona**, que **se embriaga** o hablan mal unos de otros... y siempre vamos para cumplir con el compromiso.

Ana: Es verdad. ¡Pero ésta fue una maravilla! La gente se divirtió mucho y nosotros también.

Ramón: Yo creo que los novios nunca saben lo que hacen al invitar a tanta gente.

Ana: ... Es que tienen sus compromisos personales (Ana entra al baño).

Ramón: (Caminando de lado a lado de la habitación) ¡Exacto! ¡Compromisos! ¿Por qué hay que invitar a casi toda la familia, a los vecinos y a los colegas del trabajo?

Ana: Bueno, no es obligatorio y a veces **se juntan** buenos grupos como el de hoy: la familia y los buenos amigos...

Ramón: Estos novios son viejos y **sabios**.

Ana: ¿Te parece que son viejos? ¿Por qué lo dices así?

Ramón: ¡Es que los dos ya pasan de los 30 años!

Ana: Tú tienes 35 años... ¿Crees que estás viejo? (Ana regresa a la habitación riéndose y con ropa cómoda).

Ramón: (Terminando de vestirse con ropa cómoda) Quise decir que **pudieron casarse** antes, como lo hicimos nosotros.

Ana: Sabes que ahora los novios **se la pasan bien** antes de tomar esa decisión que puede cambiar sus vidas, sus rutinas, su humor...

Ramón: Todavía hay gente que se casa temprano en la vida.

Ana: Sí... y sus matrimonios no duran mucho tiempo.

Ramón: ¡Eso no es una **ciencia** exacta! Solo hay que intentarlo y ya. ¡Míranos, vamos bien!

Ana: (**Bostezando**) Si, creo que sí.

Ramón: ¡No, no, no! No puedes tener sueño todavía. El día **aún** no termina.

Ana: Ay, vamos a dormir y ya... (Más bostezos)

Ramón: No seas **perezosa**... Vamos, tú llevas a los niños a sus camas y yo **saco al perro** a dar una vuelta.

Ana: Bueno, está bien. ¿**Despertamos** a la niñera para que sepa que ya llegamos?

Ramón: No, no. **Déjala** dormir. Ya le pagaremos mañana y la enviaremos a su casa.

Ramón: ¿Preparaste comida para mañana?

Ana: No, fue un día ocupado...

Ramón: Bueno, les daremos dinero a los niños para el **almuerzo** de mañana en el colegio.

Ana: Bueno... es que tampoco pasé por el **cajero**

automático para sacar dinero.

Ramón: ¿Y ahora? ¿Qué vamos a hacer? ¿Por qué no fuiste a buscar dinero?

Ana: Pues porque pasé el día entero en el salón de belleza...

Ramón: ¿De verdad?

Ana: Sí. Cuando hay una boda, siempre el día es largo y complicado. Los detalles de las mujeres son importantes. En el salón de belleza estaba todo el mundo: la novia, su madre, sus hermanas, la madrina y las **damas del cortejo**. Créeme, fue un día largo.

Ramón: ¡Eso es algo que nunca voy a comprender!

Ana: Hay **fechas** importantes en la vida como el día de tu boda, lleno de ilusiones, (bostezo) preparativos, (más bostezos) rituales, **amistades**, risas y **cansancio**. (Saliendo de la habitación). Voy a buscar a los niños para ponerlos en su cama y mañana seguiré explicándote.

Ramón: ¿Qué hacemos con el almuerzo de los niños?

Ana: Mañana les preparo algo **sencillo** para el

almuerzo en el colegio. Un bocadillo y una fruta.

Ramón: Ok. Voy a sacar a pasear al perro y nos vemos en un rato. Al regresar te llevaré un **sabroso** té caliente para que duermas sin interrupciones.

Ana: (Se escucha **a lo lejos**) Cuando regreses ya estaré bien dormida. Olvida el té y regresa pronto a **descansar**.

Tron (el perro): Guau... Guau... Guau...

Ramón: ¡Ya voy, Tron! ¡Vale, vale, Ana! ¡Como tú digas! (**para sí mismo**) ¡¡¡Paciencia!!!

Vocabulario

- **mascota** – pet
- **poner a un lado** – to put aside
- **asistir a** – to attend
- **un buen rato** – quite a while, a good while
- **ponerse cómodo** – to get comfortable
- **sillón** – armchair, sofa
- **quitarse** – to take off (clothes)
- **corbata** – tie
- **lanzar** – to throw
- **divertirse** – to have fun
- **dudar** – to doubt
- **desconocido** – unknown
- **chismoso** – gossipy
- **fanfarrón** – boastful
- **embriagarse** – to get drunk
- **juntarse** – to get together
- **sabio** – wise
- **poder** [3ª persona plural (ellos/ellas/ustedes) pretérito indicativo: *pudieron*] – can
- **casarse** – to get married
- **pasarselo bien** [*colloquial*] – to have a good time
- **ciencia** – science
- **bostezar** – to yawn

- **aún** – still, yet
- **perezoso** – lazy
- **sacar al perro** – to take the dog for a walk
- **despertar** – to wake up
- **déjar** – to leave, to allow
- **almuerzo** – lunch
- **cajero automático** – cash machine, ATM
- **dama del cortejo** – bridesmade
- **fecha** – date
- **amistad** – friendship
- **cansancio** – exhaustion, tiredness
- **sencillo** – simple, easy
- **sabroso** – tasty
- **a lo lejos** – in the distance, far away
- **descansar** – to rest, to sleep
- **para sí mismo** – to himself

Resumen

Ana y Ramón son una joven pareja con varios años de casados. Esta noche regresan de una boda cansados, pero contentos. Ellos conversan en su habitación mientras se cambian la ropa de gala y se ponen cómodos. Su conversación pasa por comentar acerca de la gente invitada, la comida y la bebida de la fiesta y luego hablan de lo que piensan acerca de las parejas en el mundo moderno. Luego de ponerse cómodos, se ocupan de poner a los niños en sus camas y de sacar al perro a dar un paseo. Mañana es día de trabajo para los padres y de escuela para los niños...

Preguntas de comprensión de la lectura:

1. Ana y Ramón creen que la boda fue:
    a. Una fiesta mala
    b. Una fiesta regular
    c. Una fiesta aburrida
    d. Una fiesta muy buena

2. Ana y Ramón:
    a. Tienen un gato llamado Tron
    b. Un perro llamado Tron
    c. Un gato llamado Peluche
    d. No tienen mascotas

3. Ramón piensa que las parejas deben casarse:
    a. Antes de los 20 años
    b. Antes de los 30 años
    c. Después de los 30 años
    d. Después de los 40 años

4. Ana pasó el día entero:
    a. En el supermercado
    b. En el banco
    c. En casa de su madre
    d. En el salón de belleza

5. Ana va a enviar a los niños al colegio:
   a. Con un bocadillo y una fruta para el almuerzo
   b. Con la comida que preparó para ellos
   c. Con dinero para que compren almuerzo
   d. Con la niñera

Respuestas

1. d
2. b
3. b
4. d
5. a

5. ¿CUÁNTO AZÚCAR TIENE EL YOGUR REALMENTE?

Las **tendencias** populares acerca de la salud son **poderosas**. Nos convencen de que la granola **cargada** de **jarabe de arce** es **saludable** y que cualquier cosa sin gluten es buena para todos.

Es fácil **tomar conciencia** de lo que estamos consumiendo mirando la etiqueta con la información de nutrición, pero pocas personas lo hacen. Creemos que el yogur es muy saludable por todos esos microbios beneficiosos que contiene, especialmente si es orgánico. Pero un estudio reciente **demuestra** que el yogur no siempre es tan saludable como creemos.

Investigadores en el Reino Unido estudiaron el yogur disponible en los supermercados británicos y compararon los perfiles nutricionales **de cada uno**. **Encontraron** que muchos de ellos estaban llenos de azúcar. Encontraron que el yogur orgánico, aparentemente saludable, en algunos casos contiene la **mitad** de la dosis **diaria** de azúcar recomendada.

La gente no **se da cuenta de** la cantidad de azúcar que hay en su dieta.

Los investigadores encontraron que las categorías de yogur con **sabores**, yogur con frutas o el yogur para niños, tienen contenidos **promedios** de azúcar entre 10,8 y 13 gramos por cada 100 gramos. (100 gramos son aproximadamente 3,5 onzas y una taza de yogur **estándar** en los Estados Unidos es de 5 o 5,3 onzas).

Los criterios en Estados Unidos **aconsejan** que las mujeres, o las personas con un cuerpo pequeño, mantengan en su dieta un máximo de 25 gramos de azúcar por día, y los hombres, o las personas con un cuerpo grande, unos 38 gramos por día. Los niños **deberían** consumir menos de 25 gramos al día. Esto **significa** que un solo yogur pequeño, una de las porciones que tomamos como **bocadillo**, proporciona la mitad del azúcar que necesitamos en un día.

Parte del problema es que el yogur con sabores y **endulzado** le da mala reputación al yogur natural. En este estudio, el yogur griego natural resultó mucho mejor con unos 5 gramos de azúcar por cada 100 gramos de yogur. Estos productos sin endulzar son realmente buenos para la salud, también los que se hacen con **leche entera** que son variedades con más grasa. La evidencia **sugiere** que los **productos lácteos** mejoran los lípidos en nuestra sangre. Los productos lácteos cultivados tienen bacterias vivas en su interior que contribuyen al mantenimiento de un microbioma robusto y diverso en el intestino. Pero el azúcar en todos estos yogures con sabores está **arruinando** la posibilidad de consumir una merienda saludable.

Los investigadores encontraron que el yogur orgánico tiene un poco más de azúcar que las variedades estándar, cerca de 1 gramo por cada 100 gramos de yogur. También descubrieron que las versiones **bajas en grasa** tienen menos azúcar que las variedades con toda la grasa. Muchos **medios de noticias** informaron por muchos años que los alimentos bajos en grasa tienen más azúcar para compensar la **pérdida** de sabor. Se demostró que esto es falso.

Se concluyó que los yogures griegos y los naturales son los mejores para la salud.

Esto nos deja con un problema: ¿Quién quiere comer yogur natural? Casi nadie.

Afortunadamente, usted puede **agregar** un **edulcorante** bajo en azúcares al yogur natural y tener una merienda saludable. Se hizo una prueba con una marca de yogur: se tomó un yogur con sabor a fresas y un yogur natural con unas **rebanadas** de fresa y una **cucharadita** de miel. Este último resultó, además de delicioso, tener 11 gramos menos de azúcar que el primero.

Las opciones saludables como esta, generalmente no son las más **vendidas** ni son las más baratas, pero es importante que usted esté atento a la cantidad de azúcar **oculto** en su comida. Las personas en los Estados Unidos comen un promedio de 82 gramos de azúcar todos los días. Leyó bien: 82 gramos, o aproximadamente dos o tres **veces** la cantidad que se recomienda para una vida saludable.

Cualquier cosa que podamos hacer para **disminuir** el azúcar que consumimos, más adelante significará no tener ese azúcar acumulado en el cuerpo en la forma de kilos adicionales, significará menor **riesgo** de **padecer** diabetes u otra **enfermedad** relacionada con el exceso de azúcar, significará una vida más saludable.

Consejo: ¡Leer las etiquetas con la información nutricional!

La Administración de Alimentos y Medicamentos **intenta** facilitar a los consumidores el **tener conocimiento** de lo que están comiendo, al forzar a los fabricantes a incluir en las etiquetas de nutrición los azúcares **añadidos**. Pero la decisión es de usted. **Adquiera** el hábito de leer las etiquetas y se **sorprenderá** de la cantidad de azúcar que puede eliminar de su dieta con solo estar atento.

Vocabulario

- **tendencia** – trend, movement
- **poderoso** – powerful, influential
- **cargado** – loaded, packed with
- **jarabe de arce** – maple syrup
- **saludable** – healthy
- **tomar conciencia** [+de] – to become aware, to realize
- **demostrar** – to prove, to show
- **de cada uno** – of each
- **encontrar** – to discover, to find
- **mitad** – half
- **diario** – daily
- **darse cuenta de** – to realize, to realise
- **sabor** – flavor, flavour, taste
- **promedio** – average
- **estándar** – standard
- **aconsejar** – to advise
- **deber** [3ª persona plural (ellos/ellas/ustedes) condicional indicativo: *deberían*] – have to, must
- **significar** – to indicate, to signify
- **bocadillo** – snack
- **endulzado** – sweetened
- **leche entera** – whole milk, full-cream milk
- **sugerir** – to suggest, to recommend

- **productos lácteos** – dairy products
- **arruinar** – to ruin, to destroy
- **bajo en** – low, low in
- **grasa** – fat
- **medios de noticias** – news media
- **pérdida** – loss, stripping
- **agregar** – to add
- **edulcorante** – sweetener
- **rebanada** – slice, piece
- **cucharadita** – teaspoonful, teaspoon
- **vendido** – sold
- **oculto** – hidden
- **vez** [pl: *veces*] – time(s)
- **disminuir** – to reduce, to decrease
- **riesgo** – risk, danger
- **padecer** – to suffer, to develop
- **enfermedad** – illness, disease
- **intentar** – to try, to attempt
- **tener conocimiento** – to be aware, to have knowledge
- **añadido** – added
- **adquirir** – to acquire
- **sorprender** – to get surprised, to surprise

Resumen

La publicidad nos hace creer que algunas cosas sí son saludables y la verdad es que no lo son. Una de esas creencias es que todos los yogures son saludables. Lo cierto es que el yogur natural sí es muy saludable. El yogur natural no tiene azúcar añadido, ni frutas procesadas endulzadas, ni sabores artificiales cargados de endulzantes dañinos. También es verdad que el yogur natural tiene muchos microbios beneficiosos para el cuerpo. Por su parte, el yogur griego también es muy bueno para nuestro cuerpo porque es muy alimenticio – tiene muchas proteínas – pero, hay que comprar la versión natural también. El artículo afirma que los yogures endulzados contienen la mitad del azúcar que un adulto debe consumir. Es mejor leer siempre las etiquetas y saber qué vamos a consumir.

Preguntas de comprensión de lectura

1. La lectura dice que el yogur
   - a. Es siempre saludable
   - b. Nunca es saludable
   - c. Puede tener muchas malas bacterias
   - d. Es mejor para la salud en su versión natural

2. La lectura afirma que poca gente
   - a. Lee las etiquetas de los alimentos
   - b. Come azúcar
   - c. Sabe qué es la leche entera
   - d. Tiene un cuerpo grande

3. Los yogures pueden ser malos para la salud porque
   - a. No tienen azúcar
   - b. No tienen leche
   - c. Tienen mucha azúcar
   - d. Tienen etiquetas de contenido

4. Un solo yogur endulzado puede tener
   - a. Entre 10 y 13 gramos de azúcar
   - b. El doble de lo que debe consumir una mujer adulta en un día
   - c. El doble de lo que debe consumir un hombre adulto en un día

d. La proteína de todo un día para un hombre muy grande

5. El artículo sugiere que
    a. Es mejor comprar yogur con fruta
    b. Es mejor no comprar yogur
    c. Es mejor comprar yogur natural y ponerle fruta natural
    d. Es mejor comprar yogur para niños

Respuestas

1. d
2. a
3. c
4. a
5. c

Conclusion

We hope that this book has entertained you and deepened your appreciation for Spanish. By reading these short stories, hopefully, you are capable of understanding the language a bit better. Remember that learning doesn't stop here. If you just started studying Spanish now, there's still a long way to go.

The most effective way to learn fast is to practice with a native. If no one's close to you, then connect with someone online. There are plenty of decent websites where you can find conversation partners. Most native Spanish speakers would also like to learn English. Take advantage of this opportunity to help each other out.

Make learning a part of your everyday life. Create opportunities for you to practice. How about writing your journal in Spanish? Or switching the language settings of your computer or cell phone into Spanish? Set aside a time of your day for serious studying. With consistent effort, you'll be able to master the language in no time.

Again, thank you for buying this book. If you enjoyed it, we'd like to ask you for a favor – could you leave a review for this book? It'd be really appreciated!

Thank you!

¡Buena suerte! (Good luck!)

Bonus – 10 Free Exercises

We've compiled ten exercises for you, two for each story: the first exercise will allow you to ingrain new vocabulary you will acquire through each story, while the second one focuses on grammar points that are relevant at the beginner's level A1/A2. At the end of each exercise, there are also the correct answers.

Instructions For Downloading The Free Exercises

To download the exercises, go to the following link:

http://bit.ly/free-spanish-exercises

(You should access the link on your smartphone or computer to view to or download the exercises.)

On the dedicated site, please enter your email address and your name. Then, click "DOWNLOAD".

Go to the inbox of the email address you've just entered. Find the email sent from Bono Digital with the subject "Please Confirm Your Subscription". If you cannot find the email, please also check your Spam or Promotions folders.

Once you've confirmed your email address by clicking the button "CONFIRM YOUR EMAIL", you will receive a new email with the subject line "Here are your free Spanish exercises!". Clicking the link in the email (or the picture of the book) will instantly give you access to your free exercises!

You can do the exercises immediately or you can download the file by clicking the download button (in the upper right-hand corner) and print it, if you wish.

If you encounter any problems, you can contact us at **info@bonodigital.com** – we'll do our best to help you out.

www.ingramcontent.com/pod-product-compliance
Lightning Source LLC
LaVergne TN
LVHW091343190726
843491LV00002B/854

* 9 7 8 3 9 8 2 2 6 9 2 7 6 *